PEACE BE UNTO YOU

By:

Carol Logan Patitu, Ph.D.
Professor
Buffalo State College
Department of Educational Foundations

Note for Librarians: a cataloguing record for this book that includes Dewey Decimal Classification and US Library of Congress numbers is available from the Library and Archives of Canada. The complete cataloguing record can be obtained from their online database at:
www.collectionscanada.ca/amicus/index-e.html
ISBN 1-4120-3979-7
Printed in Victoria, BC, Canada

Offices in Canada, USA, Ireland, UK and Spain
This book was published *on-demand* in cooperation with Trafford Publishing. On-demand publishing is a unique process and service of making a book available for retail sale to the public taking advantage of on-demand manufacturing and Internet marketing. On-demand publishing includes promotions, retail sales, manufacturing, order fulfilment, accounting and collecting royalties on behalf of the author.
Book sales for North America and international:
Trafford Publishing, 6E–2333 Government St.,
Victoria, BC V8T 4P4 CANADA
phone 250 383 6864 (toll-free 1 888 232 4444)
fax 250 383 6804; email to orders@trafford.com
Book sales in Europe:
Trafford Publishing (UK) Ltd., Enterprise House, Wistaston Road Business Centre,
Wistaston Road, Crewe, Cheshire CW2 7RP UNITED KINGDOM
phone 01270 251 396 (local rate 0845 230 9601)
facsimile 01270 254 983; orders.uk@trafford.com
Order online at:
www.trafford.com/robots/04-1786.html

10 9 8 7 6 5 4

Picture on Cover Page

I had a very interesting crosscultural experience in June, 2000.
My husband is originally from Tanzania. My son and I had never
met his family until a visit there in June of 2000. His family lives
in the village of Bujesi, Masoko, about 90 miles South of Mbeya,
Tanzania. The tribe is Wanyakyusa, and they speak Kinyakyusa.
We stayed in the village one night and continued visiting them for
several more days from a hostel in Mbeya as we interacted with
friends of my husband. Staying that night in the village was so
unique. I felt like I was hundreds of years back in time and we truly
enjoyed it. The village was so gorgeous and everyone was so nice.
It was such a primitive, peaceful, and heavenly environment. Such
huts are built by young boys about the age of 15, and they use the
huts as a place of exclusion, away from the control of their parents
as they pave their way into their manhood and independence.
My son and I did not speak the language, but we communicated
extremely well through hand and facial expressions. It was very hard
leaving my mother-in-law (my father-in-law is deceased). It was
an experience to cherish. The picture on the cover page was taken
during our visit right where my husband grew up in the village. It
was truly a place of peace.

In Memory of Joseph Lewis Logan, Sr.
April 2, 1938 - August 27, 1996

Loving husband, father, father-in-law, grandfather, great-grandfather, brother, brother-in-law, uncle, great uncle, friend, hard worker, neighbor, man of God, Joseph you were all these things. And everyone tied to you in one role or another deeply misses you. We really miss you more because everything is not the same. We miss your contagious smile and laughter on holidays; the goodness of your heart; your forgiving soul; your everlasting, unconditional love; your "tickling"; your joking honesty; your special barbecue sauce at picnics; your joking on Friday evenings; and your kisses and hugs on many other formal and informal occasions and gatherings at home and work. We cannot touch you, but we think of you everyday as you watch over us. We are glad you are resting in the hands of God. You are an angel looking over us. We can only rest peacefully. Everyone who crossed your path was deeply touched by your spirit and love. You are still with us, and we are still with you. And we are always checking on you.

Acknowledgements

I thank my loving husband Tony Patitu for his support as I worked on my poems. I am grateful for his honest and invaluable feedback and insight. I also thank my sister, Barbara Parker, for her thoughts on my poems as well as her suggestions for appropriate Bible verses for my religious poems. She's a true Christian. Additionally, I wish to thank my sons, Anthony and Madiba Patitu, who are such inspirations. They remind me daily of the importance of life. Their hugs and kisses are fulfilling. And I thank my late father, Joseph Lewis Logan, Sr., and my mother, Julia Logan, for their religious upbringings. It's an eternal, invaluable gift that a parent can give to a child. I thank my other siblings Lora Troutman, Joseph Logan, Jr., Jeff Logan, and Margaret Logan for their unconditional love and warm hugs. They are real, every day, loving, hard-working people whom I truly admire. And I thank my host of loving nieces and nephews who are full of spirit and determination. I thank all other family members for being who they are. God Bless.

Overview of Poetry Book

This is a poetry book expressing a depth of emotion as it explores life's many facets including childhood memories, children, death, family, father, health, life, love, motherhood, oppression, religion, responsibility, and time. All of the poems are based on my own personal experiences. The poems on children are written based on my personal experiences with my two children; and those on family are based on my experiences with family members. Also, all on "father" are about my father. The poems on oppression are based on my experiences while living in South Africa with my family in 2000. I wrote many with a religious theme because of my strong religious values. I started going to church as a child and was baptized as a child. There are several, inspiring poems written by my son, Anthony.

Table of Contents

CHILDHOOD
MEMORIES

Playing with Mother Nature

Clover, clover come to me
Playing as a child with siblings and cousins in the backyard of
grandma's pink house
Eating grapes off the vine and berries on the bushes
Sitting against the orange, brick fire grill
Standing like a fire place with its very own back

Going next door to the little brown house, also grandma's
Playing with green leaves that served as dollar bills
Next to the yard an alley full of rocks that served as our coins
Cigarette boxes filled with money – green leaves and rocks
Shopping during the summer and fall until we dropped,
exchanging money

Then came winter with snow and ice
As children, making snow huts and living in them during the day
Lighting matches in our snow huts to warm our hands
Behind the house across the street was a big field
Which filled up with water and froze
A lovely outdoor skating rink
Sliding as if we were ice skating and racing against each other
Turning boxes into sleighs
Taking a break to make snow shakes out of snow, milk and sugar
Using snow as soon as it fell
Before becoming dirty with car smoke, chimney smoke, foot prints
and dog urine

Then came spring with the rain
Not singing rain, rain go away, come back another day
Instead wishing it would pour and pour until big floods came
In streets covered with water, we ran outside, barefoot and all
Jumping in the pools of rain
All kids on the street jumping in a pool of rain and splashing each
other

As spring ended, rain brought flowers and four-leaf clovers
Smelling and picking flowers, spending a whole afternoon looking
for four-leaf clovers
Hoping for good-luck
Always looking, always wanting luck

Each season brought so much fun
Nature was our best friend
Providing all the toys we needed as children
Rocks, leaves, sticks, snow, ice and rain
Our best toys and they were free
Never thinking of real toys
We were poor and didn't even know it.

Scars

Narrow elevated scar on neck
Old-fashioned hot comb
Dropped on my neck
Slipped from the hands of my oldest sister
I a child, she an older child

Smooth scar in the middle of right leg
Falling as a little child
On the edge of a wooden porch
Of our small two bedroom home
For a family of six
Four children in one room
Parents and two small children in other room

Slender perfectly shaped scar
On back left leg
Catching the burning side
Of a hot old-fashioned stove
In the middle of the room

Scars from childhood, scars for life

Small lightly spotted scar
On inner lower right knee
From metal spokes
On the end of a college sofa bed

Scar from young adulthood, scar for life

Scars, history of events
Painful recollections
Painful beauty

Sugar Bread

A hamburger split between two of us
And a half order of fries
Snow shakes made of snow and milk
Crackers topped with peanut butter

Berries picked from bushes in the alley
Apples picked from the trees in the fields nearby
Grapes from the vines in the backyard

Beans, beans, and more beans
Kool-aid, kool-aid, and more kool-aid
Rhubarb, rhubarb, and more rhubarb

Sugar water -- nothing but water and sugar
Sugar milk -- nothing but milk and sugar
Sugar bread -- nothing but bread with sugar sprinkled on top

As six children, two brothers and four sisters, we ate all of these
things, especially the sugar bread when there was nothing else to eat
-- only bread and sugar on the kitchen counter.

That Wooden Porch

I have never forgotten about that wooden porch.
I was only a child -- a very little child.
We lived next door to Grandma's pink house.
Our house was small.
It only had 2 bedrooms, a front room and a kitchen.
Our family of 8 lived there -- mops and pops and six little children.

That house had old-fashioned siding made of tar and gray, shiny shingles.
Leading to the house was a cemented sidewalk
The kind that don't exist anymore.
There was one step leading up to that porch -- one cement step and a wooden porch.
A little one like me had to virtually jump to get to the top.
I don't know why there weren't two or three steps -- just one step.
I don't even see how an adult got from the bottom to the top with ease.

Wanting to go inside, one day I went for the leap from the step to the wooden porch.
I lifted one leg, my right leg -- oh my, I missed.
As my little brown leg came down, I scrapped it along the sharp edge of the splitting wooden porch – ouch!
I felt the painful sting and then saw the whiteness of flesh overcome with blood.
My God, that was sharp wood.
Blood just flowed down.

How can I ever forget about that wooden porch.
It left a scar in the middle of my right leg.
I see it everyday.

CHILDREN

A Child from God

A child is better than a vacation.
A child is better than a day at the beach.
A child is better than an ice cream sundae.
A child is better than a walk.
A child is better than the light summer breeze.
A child is better than a day of shopping.
A child is better than sunshine.

A child is sunshine.
A child is a breath of fresh air.
A child is better than anything. Thank you God.

Birth of a Son

Great-grand son of a West Virginian coal miner man
Great-grand son of a West Virginian Native American woman
Great-grand son of a Georgia-born Christian slave man who
migrated North
Great-grand son of a Georgia-born slave woman who migrated
North
Great-grand son of two South African born Christian men who
lived under Apartheid
Great-grand son of two South African born Christian women who
lived under Apartheid

Grandson of a West-Virginia-born, Ohioan lived blue-collar
Christian man
Grandson of a Georgia-born, Ohioan raised blue-collar Christian
woman
Grandson of a South African born Christian man who migrated to
Tanzania
Grandson of a South African born Christian woman who migrated
to Tanzania

Son of a South African born Tanzanian-raised white-collar
Christian man
Son of a Ohioan born white-collar Christian woman

Son of diversity
Son of great strength
Son of the world
Son of progression

Son full of history
Son full of beauty
Son full of love
Son full of the Holy Spirit

Birth of a Son

This is a picture of children of the Patitu family in the village of Bujesi, Masoko. The child holding the soccer ball, made of banana leaves, is Anthony Ephraim Patitu, II, son of the author.

Did I Have My Child Too Late?

I'm 36, my child is 5.
Will I see my child make it to high school?
Will I see my child's sixteen birthday?
Will I see my child get through peer pressure?
Will I see my child graduate from high school?
Will I see my child go to college?
Will I see my child graduate from college?
Will I see my child get married?
Will I see my child with my grandchildren?

Did I have my child too late?
And should I have another child?

If Our Children Knew

If our children knew their ancestors, their African brothers and sisters, were abused and split up during slavery, would they appreciate and embrace their brothers and sisters today?

If our children knew Rosa Parks refused to give up her seat to a white bus rider so they could sit where they want on a bus, would they appreciate public transportation?

If they knew individuals protested for their rights to be served in a public place and abused mentally and physically in the process, would they appreciate the luxury of eating out?

If they knew individuals, including little children, fought and died for them to attend any school, would they be more studious and be proud of being called a "nerd"?

If they knew individuals fought and died for them to have voting rights, would they take the time to vote?

If they knew individuals fought for them to have fair housing, would they appreciate their property?

If they knew individuals fought for them to have equal pay, would they not be wasteful with their money?

If they knew marchers of all ages protested, marched, and endured bombings demanding an increase of employment of African Americans, would they work wholeheartedly and value the opportunity to work?

If our children knew Dr. Martin Luther King, Jr., fought and died, for their rights, would they abuse them?

If they knew their great-grandparents and grandparents were

humiliated and harassed throughout their lives, would they caress them, respect them, listen to their words of advice, and tell they how much they love them?

If they knew God and that his son Jesus died for our sins, would they turn to him instead of drugs, gangs, or even suicide?

Mommie, I'm Not Scared, Am I?

Mommie, I'm not scared of staying in my room at night, am I?
No honey, you're not scared. The stuffed animals and beanie babies
will protect you, and I will hold your hand.

Mommie, I'm not scared of getting a shot, am I?
No honey, you're not scared. It's real quick; and you will barely feel
it.

Mommie, I'm not scared of getting my teeth cleaned, am I?
No honey, you're not scared. It will happen so fast; and it'll be over
with before you know it.

Mommie, I'm not scared to get my hair cut, am I?
No honey, you're not scared. And you will not have to get your hair
combed every day.

Mommie, I'm not scared to learn how to swim, am I?
No honey, you're not scared. Mommie will be right there to watch
you.

Mommie, I'm not scared to eat green peas, am I?
No honey, you're not scared. They will help you grow and be a big
kid.

Mommie, I'm not scared to sing in the children's choir, am I?
No honey, you're not scared. It's a piece of cake. Everyone will love
you.

Written by Anthony Ephraim Patitu, II and His Mommie, Carol
Logan Patitu

My Child

My child is five years old.
My child is close to my soul.
My child is worth more than gold.
I would never put my child on hold.

My child gives me strength morning, noon, and night.
Amidst the darkness, my child is my light.
My child has so much energy and is full of might.
With my child I can endure any plight.
My child is my loveliest sight.

My child is warm in my arms.
I try to protect my child from harm.
My child is such a charm.
In the mornings he acts as my alarm.

My child means so much to me.
I'm glad I have my child when I am weak.

My child, my child, my child.

My Child Has

My child has gorgeous, creamy, dark brown African skin;
A slim child-like boyish body;
Cute, short, fat fingers;
Straight, slender tightly fit toes;
Appealing, kinky black short hair;
Dark brown, loving, inquisitive eyes;
Glistening, straight white teeth;
A bright, cheerful, loving, welcoming big smile;
A short, friendly wide nose;
And a charismatic, embracing personality.
My child is me.

My Ebony Son

Ebony Son
Solid but soft
Dark brown with a glow
Eyes of pearl
Nose of statue
Smile of love
Heart full of kindness
Energy of welcome
Hands of courtesy and respect
My Ebony Son
My African Prince

My Five Year Old Son's Prayer

Dear God,

I pray that You watch over my dog "Bookie" and my pa pa in Heaven.
I pray I get no tallies in school.
I pray I don't have bad dreams.
I pray I get a good night's sleep.
I pray I make it to my mommy's and daddy's room if I wake up.
I pray that You watch over everyone. Amen.

O give thanks unto the Lord: for He is good: for his mercy endureth forever. Psalms 136:1.

DEATH

Before I Die

Before I die, I want to have the job I really want to do.
Before I die, I really want to go to church regularly.
Before I die, I want to tell my parents and child I love them.
Before I die, I want to visit other places I always wanted to see.
Before I die, I want to sit outside and smell the flowers and listen to the birds.
Before I die, I want to write my life's history.
Before I die, I want to visit my grandparents' gravesides.
Before I die, I want to thank God for everything I have.

But it's too late, I can't walk, I can't talk, I'm dying.

Do It Before It's Too Late

If you want to do something for someone, do it.
If you want to hug someone, do it.
If you want to kiss someone, do it.
If you want to give someone a present, do it.
If you want to help someone, do it.
If you want to give someone words of wisdom, do it.
If you want to tell someone he is doing something wrong, do it.
If you want to just spend some time talking to someone, do it.
If you want to tell someone, "I love you," do it.
If you want to tell someone about God, do it.
If it is in your heart, do it before it is too late.

Slow Death

Beer
Liquor
Everyday

Cigarettes
Inhale and exhale
On the hour

Pig feet, chitlins
Ham hocks, fat back
Pork chops
Every week

No walking, no running
Just there
No where

Slow, fat living
Slow death

FAMILY

Family Is Family, Blood Is Blood

Great-grandparents
Parents
Uncles
Aunts
Brothers
Sisters
Cousins
Children
Nieces
Nephews

Prostitutes
Pimps
Drug dealers
Drug users
Drunks
Adulterers
Liars
Troublemakers

All members of the family
All members of the family

Blood is blood
Blood is blood

Pray for each other
Help each other

Depend on God
Work in the name of God

Family passing through
Family in Hell

Family in Heaven

Family is family
Blood is blood

Behold, how good and how pleasant it is for brethren to dwell together in unity! Psalms 133:1.

How Do I Feel About My Brother?

My brother never maintained a clean room.
　　But I love him.
My brother never got good grades.
　　But I love him.
My brother graduated from high school with poor reading and writing abilities.
　　But I love him.
My brother never liked to work.
　　But I love him.
My brother now works in a fast-food restaurant as a laborer at the age of 37.
　　But I love him.
My brother explored drugs.
　　But I love him.
My brother had 3 kids but only raises one.
　　But I love him.
My brother lives in someone else's house along with his oldest son with many other people.
　　But I love him.
My brother hangs around with people from another world.
　　But I love him.
My brother does not take good care of himself and he really looks bad.
　　But I love him.
My brother does not go to church.
　　But I love him.
My brother refuses to grow up and take responsibility.
　　But I love him.
How do I feel about my brother?
I love him and he loves me. And if he could, he would do anything for me. That's my brother.

Lord, Please Don't Take My Sister

My youngest sister, age 34, is very ill;
Everyday my sister takes 22 or more pills.

I speak with her every week;
Because I know she's tired and weak.

But I know the Lord is by her side;
In the morning, noon, and night.

I pray He gives her the strength to wake up from day to day;
And I pray He takes her pain away.

I do not want my sister to suffer;
Please God, don't make it tougher.

I wish I could put her shoes on and she mine;
Because I do not want her to pass from this period of time.

Lord, please share with us the cure for AIDS:
I don't want my sister to leave this way.

Lord, please don't take my sister.
Lord, please don't take my sister.

My Ancestors

My African ancestors were captured and enslaved miles away
From villages where family was every babe.

They were captured, branded, packaged, transported, sold and
exchanged like goods
Their destination was unknown.

The year and time are unknown
From a part of Africa also unknown.

Were they Xhosa, Zulu, Masaai or what tribal group?
I do not know from where my ancestors were swooped.

They were for sure African and taken against their will
Which when I think about it, it gives me more than the chills.

I wonder what life would have been like
If Europeans had not colonized Africa and caused so much dislike.

Would I have been one of many HIV/AIDS victims trying to raise
my children
In an inefficient system?

Would I have been a South African in exile during Apartheid
From the government's fear and lies?

Would I have been a domestic worker in a white person's house
Or dead as a freedom fighter from a fire douse?

Would I have been living freely
But locked up in the apartheid mentality?

Would I have been a renowned and highly respected leader who
fought against Apartheid and other forms of captivity

That eventually led Blacks to victory?

Would I have been living in poverty in the West Coast of Africa or
some other parts
With the love of my children shining through in my heart?

Would I have been a victim of the tribal wars
In Rwanda, Burundi or in the Democratic Republic of Congo left
with scars?

Would I have been unemployed or underemployed after being
educated
Going into despair and being unable to contribute feeling
suffocated?

Would I have been living in a squatter camp
With my clothes all damp and a makeshift fire not even a lamp?

Would I only have had to eat bread and water
Or not even that, only to hear my children's poverty hollers?

Would I have been a true African leader
Serving interests of the masses as a true born leader?

Would I have been an African Queen
Married to an African King?

Only God knows what I would have been.
I just know that my culture is used to a physical or verbal fight for
their rights
All around the world day and night.

Oppressed
Oppressed
Oppressed
From one generation to the next.

Africa has been bleeding.
Africans have been fighting back for so long.

When will it end?
When will it end?
When will it truly end?

My Grandfather

Hard-working, dark-skinned, well-dressed slender man
With tough, yet tender-looking hands

A man of God
Amidst the odd

Singing spirituals from the soul
Unknowingly life taking its toll

Caring for three children and a wife
Making the most out of life

Migrating with his family in the late 40s from Georgia to Ohio
To get away from the Ku Klux Klan that haunted him since a child

He took care of his family in a two-story pink house in a small
Ohioan town
His children and first grandchildren by his side he never frowned.

He was high-spirited and happy
Full of love, a true loving pappy.

I never got to meet him; I was a year late,
But I knew him from mother's tales.

My grandfather died at the age of forty-six
I can only ask why.

A single massive heart attack took him away from here a year before
I was born
But he will always be thought of in a heart untorn.

My Itching Foot

My itching foot
My itching foot
My itching foot
All weekend but never before

My youngest sister, terminally ill, was not feeling well.
My mother kept saying how she could tell.

My sister was breathing deep,
And kept wanting to sleep.

I called her from Texas, she was in Ohio.
She was glad to hear from me and my child.

We talked but soon she wanted to get off the phone.
Something was wrong, she never had this tone.

She kept telling my mother she was tired.
Her poor soul was burning with fire.

She had been visiting home all weekend.
But Sunday, it was time for her to return to Cleveland.

Over the next few days, I kept thinking about her.
I couldn't get her off of my mind, that was for sure.

Late Wednesday evening after eleven o'clock,
I got a call from my mother, she was in shock.

She said, "I don't want to scare you but Margaret had a seizure."
I pulled myself together, and thought, "Lord, don't leave her."

All I could think of was poor, poor thing.
She had been through so many things.

My mother hung up but would be calling me back.
I was afraid to go to sleep, not knowing if I would need to pack.

My itching foot
My itching foot
My itching foot
Why all over again?

At 1:00 a.m. I decided to go to bed.
Waiting for my mother's call was making me really sad.

I had a very hard time of falling to sleep.
I was thinking of my sister who must be really weak.

That morning I woke up wondering if something went wrong.
Praying to God and singing a church song.

Finally, I learned that my sister was OK in a hospital bed.
I was so relieved that she was not dead.

They were doing tests to determine the cause.
In the meantime I exhaled and took a pause.

No itching foot
No itching foot
No itching foot

Oh, How I Miss Home

Oh, how I miss home.
I miss my conversations with my parents and falling to sleep on them or them on me.
Oh, how I miss home.
I miss seeing my brothers and sisters -- talking, arguing, debating, laughing and crying with them.
Oh, how I miss home.
I miss the smiling faces of nieces and nephews -- and their hugs and kisses and their fights with each other.
Oh, how I miss home.
I miss the family gatherings on Friday evenings at my parents home.
Oh, how I miss home.
I miss the fussing and happy cussing.
Oh, how I miss home.
I miss Tubby's pizza -- the cheapest and best in town.
Oh, how I miss home.
I miss my father's homemade barbecue sauce at picnics and other family gatherings.
Oh, how I miss home.
I miss all the home-cooked meals for Labor Day, Memorial Day and other holidays -- everything made from scratch.
Oh, how I miss home.
I miss the special family events -- graduations and weddings.
Oh, how I miss home.
I miss the shopping sprees with my sisters and cousins.
Oh, how I miss home.
I miss other family members and friends.
Oh, how I miss home.
I miss church in my hometown on Sunday mornings, the choir singing, and the inspiring energy-filled sermons of our Baptist preacher.
Oh, how I miss home.
I miss the change of seasons -- fall, winter, spring and summer --

fall colored leaves, snow, spring flowers, and nice warm, bearable summer temperatures.
I look forward to going home.

Ruin the Pot

Onions
Tomatoes
Carrots
Corn
Cabbage
Beef

A great tasting pot of soup
Add more tomatoes
A rotten tomato
Ruin the pot, ruin the pot

Grandfather
Grandmother
Father
Mother
Brothers
Sisters

A great family reunion
Add more relatives
A distant trouble-making cousin
Ruin the pot, ruin the pot

The Best Home

Condominium home
Log cabin home
Patio home
Suburban home
Urban home
Country home
Lake home
Historical home
Estate home
Vacation home
The best home is the Christian home and the Church home,
leading to the heavenly home.

This is none other but the house of God, and this is the gate of
Heaven. Genesis 28:17.

The Black Sheep

The Black Sheep
À distant member of the family
Suppose to be

He speaks through others
Never through his own words.

He complains about anything good
As he plans to tear the positive apart
And knocks others down.

He is not seen for many, many years;
One does not even know his evil works
Until years of destruction.

When the destruction is done,
He may not be able to resist the temptation
To be known and take a bow.

But even when he quickly and only once identifies himself,
He continues to use others to do his dirty work.

Once the family members know his evil works,
They are surprised to know the Black Sheep
For he has hugged them for years and said, "Cous, I love you."

All alone he hated their guts and despised them,
And said negative things about them,
And sabotaged their good works.

Once he is fully known,
He is even worse than before
As he attempts to finish his evil works to final destruction.

Glad that he has been fully exposed,
He takes great joy in seeing others suffering in pain
In learning not only his evil works but who he is.

The Black Sheep
Not really a relative
But the devil in disguise
Not a "cous"
But a was

The Strongest One in the Family

Of six children the oldest is Lora, now 42 years of age.
She's married and has three grown daughters.
In spite of her childbearing years she's thin as can be --- only 120
pounds.
How can someone so thin carry so much weight?
She solves all the family problems.

She has helped to raise one of my brother's children.
She lets any family member in need stay at her home
She gives money to family in need no matter how bad she needs it.
She's forever buying things for the little ones in the family.
She stores items of family members in her garage as needed.

She lets any out-of-town visiting family members stay at her house.
She calls and checks on everyone.
She organizes our family gatherings.
She fulfills multiple tasks and roles in our hometown church and in
community organizations.

For someone so thin, she carries so much weight.
She keeps the family together through her heart which weighs more
than her whole body.
As the strongest one in the family, she's very special.

Uncle Jim

Uncle Jim, the only uncle we knew
Nice, caring personality
Very big, heavy-set body of strength
Clothes too tight
Yellowish brown skin
Hardworking blue-collar man
Always saying, "Sounds like a personal problem to me."

Uncle Jim always liked to drink
No matter what day of the week
He went straight to my dad's bar room when he came over
He would drink anything, especially "hard" liquor
One glass after another with no water to wash it down
Followed by smoking

Year after year after year went by
Uncle Jim is now tired and weak
A limping body
Feet swollen with gout
High blood pressure
A slouchy body, diminished in size with clothes just hanging
The drinking and smoking have taken their toll on his body
We know he's ill but he will not go to the doctor
He doesn't want to know what we already know
Or he just doesn't care
God, carry him home.

This is a family photo of Anthony Ephraim Patitu, Sr., and Carol Logan Patitu with children Anthony Ephraim Patitu, II, and Madiba Joseph Patitu, on mother's lap.

This is a photo of Carol Patitu's family. Seated from left to right: Carol Patitu, father Joseph Lewis Logan, Sr., mother Julia Elizabeth Logan, and sister Barbara Parker. Standing from left to right: siblings Lora Troutman, Jeff Logan, Margaret Logan, and Joseph Logan, Jr.

This is a family photo taken in the village of Bujesi, Masoko about 90 miles South of Mbeya, Tanzania. Seated from left to right: Carol Patitu; son Anthony Patitu, II; Njasi Kipesile Patitu, mother; Ruth Kilasa Patitu, sister-in-law; and Anthony Patitu, Sr.

This is a photo of some members of the Patitu family in the village of Bujesi, Masoko about 90 miles South of Mbeya, Tanzania. The tribe is Wanyakyusa, and they speak Kinyakyusa. On his knee in the front row is Anthony Ephraim Patitu, II, son of the author.

FATHER

Father Full of Love

Slender head
With winning smile, straight white teeth
Light mustache
Smooth friendly cheeks
Wide pear shape nose
Charismatic, loving eyes
Smooth eyebrows
Soft, short salt and pepper hair
Light caramel skin
Medium frame, tall body
With coal miner and factory hands, tough and strong yet gentle

Full of joy and happiness
Full of friendship
Full of soul
Full of forgiveness
Full of giving
Full of thanks
Full of religion
Full of love
Full of kindness
Full of energy
Full of charity
Full of spirit

My father was so sweet.
He worked hard every week.
He wanted to retire at the age of sixty.
But now he's deceased,
Dead at the age of fifty-eight.
He's now through the Heavenly gate,
The best retirement of all.

Love in honor of my father.

I Love Black Men

My ancestors were Black.
My great-grandfathers were Black.
My grandfathers were Black.
My father was Black.
My minister is Black.
Male mentors were Black.
My close male friends are Black.
My husband is Black.
My sons are Black.

I love Black men.

The late Joseph Lewis Logan, Sr., father of Carol Logan Patitu

My Father

My father drove the church bus.
   My father is in me.
My father worked two jobs.
   My father is in me.
My father bought me shoes and clothes.
   My father is in me.
My father played with me.
   My father is in me.
My father kissed, hugged and tickled me.
   My father is in me.
My father said, "I love you".
   My father is in me.
My father loved me unconditionally.
   My father is in me.
My father was always happy.
   My father is in me.
Don't talk about my father.
Because my father is in ME!

My Father's Hands

Firm as oak
Gentle as cotton
Flowing as water

My father's hands, always there

He carried me as a child with his hands.
He tickled me as a child with his hands.
He disciplined me as a child with the motions of his hands.
He prayed with me with his hands.
He patted me on the head with his hands.
He hugged me with his hands.

My father's hands, always there

Those big, strong, caramel, vein-filled manly hands, always there

My father is gone.
But I still see and feel my father's hands.
Those big, strong, caramel, vein-filled manly hands, always there

Thank you God for leaving the memories of my father's hands.
They comfort me and guide me everyday of my life.

My Father's Last Prayer

My father lay in the hospital bed
Not too far from being dead.

He knew he was leaving but he never cried
Being strong as he could be without asking why.

Cancer was identified in his body only eight months before
Right in his stomach deep to the core.

It was so bad they had to immediately take his stomach;
I was so distraught I could not fully comprehend it.

All we could do was hope and pray,
But we really knew what lay ahead.

When he went back into the hospital eight months later,
We became much sadder but would not turn into haters.

But we did ask why unlike our father
Who could not eat nor drink water.

His fourth morning in the hospital he was still Joseph as nice as
could be;
He still smiled at people as they passed his bed for he could see.

Not only could he see but he could slowly and shortly talk;
He was so jubilant as if he could walk.

But he could not even lift his body,
But that would not stop him from being jolly.

That afternoon only a few short hours later
He stopped talking and paying attention to bodies.

I was getting worried but I thought maybe he was just sleeping,
But unknowingly to me he was dying.

Only moments later his life came to an end,
But up above in Heaven it would begin.

My father knew he was dying, for the night before
He said a prayer to our Heavenly Father, Our Dear Lord.

For late that night before, he told me and my mother to stand by
his bed
As he said with his eyes closed and his hands clasped in prayer up to
his head:
"Lord, I hope you have trust in me, as I have trust in you."

My father's last prayer.

HEALTH

Silent Pain

Tickling toes
Crackling knees
Aching hip
Stifling fingers
Throbbing head
Closing eyes
Popping out of joint bones
Aching sides
Numbing body -- right side only from waist to head
What is this?

Silent pain from daily stressors of life

LIFE

There Is a Lesson in All Things

Behind the dark clouds, there is a silver lining.
In the midst of pain, there is a silver lining.
In the midst of frustration, there is a silver lining.
In the midst of exhaustion, there is a silver lining.
In the midst of sickness, there is a silver lining.
In the midst of sadness, there is a silver lining.
In the midst of misunderstanding, there is a silver lining.
In the midst of troubles, there is a silver lining.
In the midst of problems, there is a silver lining.
In the midst of agony, there is a silver lining.
In the midst of death, there is a silver lining.
There is a lesson in all things.

And there was a cloud that overshadowed them: and a voice came
out of the cloud, saying, This is my beloved Son: hear him. Mark 9:
7

When You're Young

When you're young,
You don't think about your health.
You don't think about your weight.
You don't think about saving for retirement.
You don't think about whether you're too old to have kids.
You don't think about moving back to your hometown.
You don't think about what you should have accomplished by now in life.
You don't think about diseases or illnesses.
You don't think about saving your soul.
You don't think about dying.

But you think about these things in your late 30s when you're faced with all these issues.

Enjoy life while you're young.

Who Fought For Me?

My ancestors fought for me.
My grandparents fought for me.
My father fought for me.
My mother fought for me.
My family fought for me.
My hometown church members fought for me.
My fifth grade teacher fought for me.
My community, national, and international leaders fought for me.
My college and professional mentors fought for me.
My colleagues fought for me.
Unsung heroes fought for me.
God fought for me and continues to fight for me.

Surely, I can fight for myself now.

You Lift Up Your Head, Smile, and Live

When people talk negatively about you
Even when you have done no wrong

When people hate and despise you
Even when you have loved them

When people envy you to no end
Even when you have given to them

When people work against you
Even when you have helped them

When people lie about you
Even when you have told the loving truth about them

When people treat you jealously for your accomplishments
Even when you have spoken highly of them

When they have done all these things,
You lift up your head, smile, and live.

They may cause you pain in your heart
But they can never take away your soul and your passion for living.

LOVE

An Expression of Love

Arms tangling
Fingers moving under the arms
Heads knocking
Mouths wide open and gasping for air
Legs tangling
Feet touching
Fingers now moving tip to tip over bodies
Neck, armpits, sides, waist, thighs, legs, and toes
Tossing and turning
Bodies rolling all over the floor
Laughing and breathing hard
Tickling, an expression of love
From my father to me
And from me to my child

Baby Love

Snuggled up against my body
His leg thrown over my thigh
Rubbing his feet above my knee
His head pressed against my shoulder
Looking up at me with a loving smile
And gorgeous romantic eyes
His arm reached up towards my head and his fingers twirling
smoothly
Through my hair over and over again
Love from my little baby boy

Unconditional Love

Unconditional love is loving someone if he does not do what you want him to do.

Unconditional love is loving someone if he does not come see you when you want him to.

Unconditional love is loving someone when he does not live up to your expectations.

Unconditional love is loving someone when he does not have your attitudes, values, and morals.

Unconditional love is loving someone when he is not the person you want him to be.

Unconditional love is loving someone without trying to control him.

Unconditional love is loving someone with no strings attached.

Unconditional love is always forgiving the person.

Unconditional love is always helping someone no matter how many times he has failed.

True love is unconditional love.

For God so loved the world, that he gave his only begotten Son, that whosoever believeth in him should not perish, but have everlasting life. John 3:16

MOTHERHOOD

Mother Hopes

Mother hopes her child will be healthy;
Mother hopes her child will take his first step;
Mother hopes her child will not get hit by a car;
Mother hopes her child will not be kidnapped;
Mother hopes her child will not get ill;
Mother hopes her child will get along with other children;
Mother hopes her child will grow up with no problems;
Mother hopes her child will get good grades throughout school;
Mother hopes her child will graduate from high school;
Mother hopes her child will stay in church;
Mother hopes her child will not do drugs nor drinking;
Mother hopes her child will not get hit by a drunk driver;
Mother hopes her child will not have a baby too early;
Mother hopes her child will go to college;
Mother hopes her child will make a decent salary;
Mother hopes her child will be able to move out on his own;
Mother hopes her child will stay close to the family;
Mother hopes her child will meet and marry a decent person;
Mother hopes her child will treat everybody right; and
Mother hopes her child will be able to live on without her when she
dies.

Why a Day for Mothers

We celebrate "Mother's Day" because:

A mother will wash clothes even on Mother's Day;
A mother will fix breakfast for her family even on Mother's Day;
A mother will make the beds even on Mother's Day;
A mother will clean her house even on Mother's Day;
A mother will attend to the needs of family and friends even on Mother's Day;
A mother will take care of things from work even on Mother's Day;
A mother will give away some food made especially for her even on Mother's Day;
A mother will take care of herself last even on Mother's Day;
That's why we celebrate a day for mothers because
Even on Mother's Day, a mother puts everything and everybody first!

OPPRESSION

Apartheid

Apartheid, alive and well
No matter where you go,
There's a story to tell.

Apartheid in South Africa ended in theory,
But is alive in practice.

First Whites
Then Indians
Then Coloureds
Then Africans – last, last, always last

The more indigenous you are
The more likely you are barred.

How did this ever happen?
It makes you so sadden.

Such kind, kind people
Just stepped on like beetles

But their day will soon come
When the struggle is won
For equal treatment, equal treatment
Not only in theory
BUT ALSO IN PRACTICE.

Apartheid & Post Apartheid

Apartheid in South Africa:

Apartheid, discrimination based on race, was legalized in 1948.
Before 1948, apartheid was practiced but the law was silent – the
air full of hate.

White government
Depressing
Painful
Blood-boiling
Black masses at the bottom
Whites on top
Black oppression
White supcriority
Black servants
White masters

Post-Apartheid in South Africa:

The "Post-Apartheid Era" began only in 1994.
The country's wealth in the hands of 10% Whites, the indigenous
were poor.

Black government
Depressing
Painful
Blood-boiling
Black masses at the bottom
Whites on top
Black oppression
White superiority
Black servants
White masters

Day to day, day to day

Real change, yet to come
Time is needed to change years, years, years of oppression.

Black Men Be Strong

Brothers killing brothers
Bullets hitting babies
When will it stop

Sons killing mama's hearts
Needing daddy's hugging hands and discipline
And encouraging words from grown Black men

Killing over drugs
Killing in their house
Killing in the hood

Hanging out in the streets
In front of liquor stores
With drugs and liquor
Waiting for a kill
Needing a mentor

Young little girls and boys
Seeing thugs and whores
Up against the Black leaders
And the preachers

Black males Black males
Always against the odds

Kidnapped – white men
Slavery – white men
Beaten and hung – white men
Drugs brought into their communities – white men
Prejudice and racism – white men

Keep fighting
Keep fighting

Keep fighting
And be strong

Never giving up
Black men be strong

Effects of Oppression

Deep breathing
Shaking knees
Frozen or silenced voice
Sadden eyes
Confused hearing
Trembling hands
Palpating heart
Chest pain
Severe, exploding headaches
Numbed body
Effects of oppression

Leave My Freedom Alone

Driveway
Automatic gate locks
Fences, high fences
Automatic lights outside
Locked in my space

Security system
Panic buttons on the walls and for the hand
If I'm attacked

Bars in front of every window
Back windows, front windows, side windows
Bar door in front of glass door
I can't see peacefully outside
Locks, locks, and more locks

Hallway door to bedrooms locks
Locked into a part of the house
Each bedroom door locks
Locked into a room

Enough is enough
Prisoner in my own home
And in a single room at night
I can't sleep

Nights of tears
My eyes are open staring out the window
Living in fear wondering are they out there
Leave my freedom alone
Let me enjoy South Africa
Leave my freedom alone.

Messages

"I didn't see you" as you're waited on last although you weren't last.
"You don't get it; you just don't get it" although you clearly did and
they don't look at you and don't want to talk with you.
"I want you to vote for another person" who is new and hasn't
arrived and thus you vote against yourself.
"I said it for you", in other words you keep quiet.
"You can't do that" although others have.
"I don't have anything against you but …"
Messages from racist people that strike like a sword.
They say anything to make you feel inferior.
Their goal is to keep you down.

"You can do whatever you want."
"You're so loving."
"We're going to do this together."
"You would be a great leader."
Messages from genuine, caring non-racist people.
They know you can do what anyone else can do.
Their goal is to move you forward or lift you up.

"We love you."
"You have such a big heart."
"You really care about others."
"I'm so proud of you."
"You're going to do great things."
"You're an angel to so many."
"One day I'm going to be like you."
Messages of love and encouragement from my African American
people who I will always need.
They admire you and are proud that you're from their community.
Their goal is to love you unconditionally and "always" be there for
you and to help you succeed.

Messages

Oppression

"I didn't see you."
But I was there waiting time and time again
To be helped even before others came in.

"I didn't hear you."
Even though I said the same thing
Before the others talking after me.

I have been ignored,
Silenced,
Left out, and
Isolated
All due to my gorgeous brown skin
That was beneath them.

And thus, I have felt inferior,
Scared,
Numb,
Insignificant,
Unwanted and
Speechless although so many thoughts were in my mind.

They never did "see" me and
They never did "hear" me.

I wanted to run and holler.
I wanted to say:
 "I am here, I am here" and
"I can talk, I can talk."

I never, never wanted to see ever again those who have caused me so
much pain;
Those who have made my heart too heavy to bear;
Those who made my knees shake;

And those who made me scared to say all that I wanted to say
Because I knew they were being judgmental
And stereotyped my every word, my every movement.

I wanted to run and run and run and run
Because it's so much to bear.

Do they realize what they're doing?
My ancestors jumped into the ocean to get away from them.
I want to run and run and cry out and ask God, "Why all dark-
skinned people 'all' around the world?"
Which I can but I got to fight for my rights
For the sake of my sons.

No more jumping in the ocean and no more running.
My sons, our sons, will be the Kings they have always been.
And our daughters will be the Queens they have always been.

Same Pain, Different Name

Haunted as a slave
Haunted as a servant
Haunted as a nigger
Haunted as a Negro
Haunted as a Colored person
Haunted as a Black person
Haunted as an Afro-American
Haunted as an African American
Same pain, different name

Slavery & Apartheid

Slavery
Apartheid

African Americans
African

Freedom fighters imprisoned
Freedom fighters imprisoned

Oppression and poverty
Oppression and poverty

Husbands separated from wives and families
Husbands separated from wives and families

Children separated from mothers and fathers
Children separated from mothers and fathers

Superiority and inferiority
Superiority and inferiority

Whites above Blacks
Whites above Blacks

End of slavery
End of apartheid

Segregated areas and ghettos
Townships and squatter camps

Blacks in poverty
Blacks in poverty

Still no real freedom

Still no real freedom

Two different countries – the United States and South Africa
People all with a historical bond
Still sharing similar experiences
Experiences that never should have been

Black movement, Black history
African Renaissance

Struggling for freedom and a place in their country
Struggling for freedom and a place in "THEIR" country

Picture of homes in a squatter camp next to Langa Township in South Africa

RELIGION

Angel Dog

My doggie passed away.
But my doggie is alive.
My doggie is an angel dog.

Written by Anthony Ephraim Patitu, II, at age six

Blessing from God

When God bless you with food, share it.
When God bless you with clothing, share it.
When God bless you with shelter, share it.
When God bless you with happiness, share it.
When God bless you with love, share it.
When God bless you with wisdom, share it.
When God bless you with His spirit, share it.
These are blessings from God, share them.

God shall bless us; and all the ends of the earth shall fear him.
Psalms 67:7

Bread: Sustenance

Bread
Sustenance
Livelihood

White bread
Rye bread
Wheat bread
Nut bread
Pumpernickel bread
Sesame seed bread
Garlic bread
Cinnamon bread

Jesus, the Bread of Life
Bread of all bread.

And Jesus said unto them, I am the bread of life: he that cometh to me shall never hunger; and he that believeth on me shall never thirst. St. John 6: 35.

Christmas and New Year Prayer

Thank you God for this day.
Thank you for letting us go to New Orleans for the Sugar Bowl
Game.

I pray that the Aggies play a good game.
I pray that the Buckeyes play a good game.

Thank you for Baby Jesus. Amen

Written by Anthony Ephraim Patitu, II, at age six

Enter into his gates with thanksgiving, and into his courts with
praise: be thankful unto him, and bless his name. Psalms 100:4

Covenant

Covenant
Agreement

Promises made to man
God to man
Man to man

Mixing of blood
Covenant
Complete

Then
Blood mixing
Strong
Unity
One

Now blood mixing
Unity but
Deadly
Diseases
Fatal

Then
Blood, symbol of strength

Now
Blood, symbol of death

Blood mixing or
Blood killing?

Dear Lord, Help Me

Dear Lord, help me take another step
    when I am tired;
Dear Lord, help me put my body in gear
    when I am stressed;
Dear Lord, help me talk to people
    when I am upset;
Dear Lord, help me to exhale
    when I am exhausted;
Dear Lord, help me to shake someone's hand
    when I don't want to;
Dear Lord, help me to smile
    when I want to frown;
Dear Lord, help me to solve a problem
    when I want to walk away;
Dear Lord, help me to say, "I don't know,"
    when I don't have the answer;
Dear Lord, help me to remember that with you,
    all things are possible.

Forsake me not, O Lord: O my God, be not far from me.
Make haste to help me, O Lord my salvation. Psalms 38: 21- 22

Feelings for All and Consideration for Life

When I think of gaieties, I think of sorrows. I am proud to be what I am, but I think about people who have no exciting life to look forward to. Many people should think about how lucky they are compared to many other people. Every time I am depressed, I think about how lucky I really am; then I feel better, but I feel bad in the heart when I think about people who are crippled, blind, speechless, helpless or worse off than myself. I also pity people who are selfish, jealous, stubborn, prejudiced, etc. If those who are able would help the helpless, life would be happier. Life could be better if there were not thieves, crooks, murderers, etc., who cause afflictions. Life is being destroyed. Will the world decline or will God take over first? Or better yet, will man communicate with man? There is always that chance because all things are possible under the eye of God.

Written by Carol Jean Logan (as a 10th grader in 1978)
Now Carol Logan Patitu
First appeared in Orb, Vol. XI, No. 1, p. 14, Marion Harding High School

This picture was taken outside of Dar-es-Salaam in Tanzania. The picture of the cross represents the starting point of Christianity in East Africa in 1868. Pictured: Carol Patitu; Anthony Ephraim Patitu, II; and Njili Mwakoba, nephew of Anthony Patitu, Sr.

God Is Our Creator

God is our Creator.
The devil is our destructor,
But we are followers of whom?

Written by Carol Jean Logan (as a 10th grader in 1978)
Now Carol Logan Patitu
First appeared in Orb, Vol. XI, No. 1, p. 15, Marion Harding High
School

In the beginning God created the heaven and the earth. Genesis 1:1

I Am a Servant

I am a servant of the handicap.
I am a servant of the sick.
I am a servant of the homeless.
I am a servant of the shut-in.
I am a servant of the weak.
I am a servant of the poor.
I am a servant of the wicked.
I am a servant of the needy.
I am a servant of the deprived.
I am a servant of the less fortunate.
I am a servant of the children.
I am a servant of others.

As we have therefore opportunity, let us do good unto all men, especially unto them who are of the household of faith. Galatians 6:10

I Wonder If God Envisioned

I wonder if God envisioned us flying through the air.
I wonder if God envisioned us walking on the moon.
I wonder if God envisioned us cruising over the ocean.
I wonder if God envisioned us speeding on the grounds.

I wonder if God envisioned us using ovens and microwaves.
I wonder if God envisioned us using cellular phones and
computers.
I wonder if God envisioned us using electric fireplaces.
I wonder if God envisioned us using washers and dryers.

I wonder if God envisioned us wearing dyed hair.
I wonder if God envisioned us wearing designer clothes.
I wonder if God envisioned us wearing diamonds and jewels.
I wonder if God envisioned us wearing make-up and sculptured
nails.

I wonder if God envisioned us being fluent in so many languages.
I wonder if God envisioned us having so many different cultures
and religions.
I wonder if God envisioned us having so many different attitudes,
behaviors, morals, and values.
I wonder if God envisioned us traveling within hours to see
someone around the world.

I wonder if God envisioned us doing so many things with His
blessings and will.
Thank you, God!

For of him, and through him, and to him, are all things: to whom
be glory for ever. Amen. Romans 11:36

I'm Going to Tell God When I Get to Heaven

Mommie, if you're bad to me, I'm going to tell God when I get to Heaven.

Mommie, if you don't feed me, I'm going to tell God when I get to Heaven.

Mommie, if you don't stay with me while I bathe, I'm going to tell God when I get to Heaven.

Mommie, if you don't put me to bed, I'm going to tell God when I get to Heaven.

Mommie, if you don't read to me at bedtime, I'm going to tell God when I get to Heaven.

Mommie, if you don't dress me in the morning, I'm going to tell God when I get to Heaven.

Mommie, if you don't play with me, I'm going to tell God when I get to Heaven.

Written by Anthony Ephraim Patitu, II, at age six

Let Me Thank God While It's on My Mind

I'm not worrying about thanking God for my house, my car, my clothes, my jewelry, my money nor any other materialistic things.

I have more crucial things to thank God for. He can take all of these things from me because he has given me more important things.

I thank him for the clean water I drink.
I am so blessed that I don't have to go to a dirty puddle or filthy river to fetch water.
I taste fresh water and not dirt water.
I thank God for clean water.

I thank God for my freedom.
My freedom to go to my car and down my driveway without worrying about getting shot in my head for my car or for pure fun for someone else.
I thank God for my freedom.

I can roam wherever I want – to work, home, the store, wherever
Without worrying about being followed, without worrying about being carjacked or murdered.
I thank God for my freedom and ability to roam.

I thank God for being able to sleep through the night
Without waking up two or three times for fear that someone is going to break into my house through our gate, fences and bushes, locks and windows with bars and regular doors as well as bar doors, a security system and a locked hallway door leading to the bedrooms and then locked bedroom doors.
I thank God for being able to sleep at night.

I thank God for my body and not worrying about anyone raping me because it's so easy for them to do it.

I thank God for my body.

I thank God for my friends everywhere I go.
Without them, without the Angels he has sent to watch over me,
I would be lost. The police would not protect me where I last was.
But I have God's Angels.
Thank you God for bringing the Angels into my life.

I thank you for fresh water, my freedom, my ability to freely roam,
my sleep at night, my body and my earthly and Heavenly Angels,
those watching over me from above.

I had to thank God while it was on my mind.

Thank you God.

Praise ye Him, sun and moon; praise Him, all ye stars of light.
Psalm 148:3.

Man's Soul Belongs to God

Man's soul belongs to God –
Like the trees, the flowers, the water, the earth, the sun, and the moon.

For ye were as sheep going astray; but are now returned unto the Shepherd and Bishop of your souls. I Peter 2:25

In the sweat of thy face shalt thou eat bread, till thou return unto the ground; for out of it wast thou taken: for dust thou art, and unto dust shalt thou return. Genesis 3:19

Overcome Evil with Good

When someone frowns at you, smile at him.
When someone says, "I hate you," say, "I love you."
When someone refuses to talk with you, say, "how are you?"
When someone refuses to shake your hand, hug him.
When someone says bad things about you, speak good things of him.
When someone refuses to help you, offer your services.
When someone refuses to see how you're doing, check on him.
When someone has a bad attitude towards you, remain calm and act positively towards him.
When someone does something hateful toward you, forgive him.
When someone acts hateful towards you, say, "I and God love you."

In time he will smile at you; say, "I love you"; say, "How are you?"; hug you; speak good things of you; offer his services; check on you; remain calm and act positively towards you; forgive you; and say, "I love you."

Be not overcome of evil, but overcome evil with good. Romans 12:21

Promises to God

I'm going to start going to church every Sunday, not every other Sunday.
I'm going to start going to Sunday School.
I'm going to start going to communion on first Sundays in the afternoon.
I'm going to start singing in the choir again.
I'm going to start going to prayer service on Wednesdays.
I'm going to start going to Bible study on Wednesdays.
I'm going to start helping with different church events.
I'm going to start visiting the sick.
I'm going to start helping those in need.

God got tired of my unfulfilled promises.
Death has come my way.

I will go into thy house with burnt offerings: I will pay thee my vows. Psalms 66:13.

I will pay my vows unto the Lord now in the presence of all his people. Psalms 116: 14.

Salvation

Momma, save me.
Momma can't save you.

Papa, save me.
Papa can't save you.

Sister, save me.
Sister can't save you.

Brother, save me.
Brother can't save you.

Cousin, save me.
Cousin can't save you.

Friend, save me.
Friend can't save you.

Grandma, save me.
Grandma can't save you.

Grandpa, save me.
Grandpa can't save you.

Christian, save me.
Christian can't save you.

Who can save me?
You have to save yourself.

Wherefore, my beloved, as ye have always obeyed, not as in my
presence only, but now much more in my absence, work out your
own salvation with fear and trembling. For it is God which worketh
in you both to will and to do of his good pleasure. Philippians 2:
12-13.

So Good

The sun feels so good.
The rain feels so good.
The wind feels so good.
The presence of the Lord feels so good.

The trees look so good.
The flowers look so good.
The mountains look so good.
The rivers look so good.
The presence of the Lord looks so good.

The birds sound so good.
The animals sound so good.
The voices sound so good.
The waterfalls sound so good.
The presence of the Lord sounds so good.

The food smells so good.
The flowers smell so good.
The grass smells so good.
The trees smell so good.
The presence of the Lord smells so good.

The Lord is so so good.

Oh, give thanks unto the Lord; for He is good; for his mercy
endureth for ever. Psalm 118:29.

The Fulfilling Fruit of All

Apples from the orchard
Bananas from the tropical plants
Berries from the bush
Grapes from the vineyard
Oranges from the citrus trees
Strawberries from the patch

Fruit of the Holy Spirit, the fulfilling fruit of all

But the fruit of the Spirit is love, joy, peace, longsuffering,
gentleness, goodness, faith, meekness, temperance; against such
there is no law. Galatians 5:22-23.

The Lord in My Life

The Lord in my life protects me from pain;
The Lord in my life gives me comfort during sorrow;
The Lord in my life gives me hope in the time of despair;
The Lord in my life gives me family and friends during times of loneliness;
The Lord in my life gives me a smile on the peak of a frown;
The Lord in my life gives me Christian fulfillness when I hunger;
The Lord in my life gives me protection when danger arises;
The Lord in my life gives me warmth against coldness;
The Lord in my life provides me patience during difficulty times;
The Lord in my life provides me understanding during times of decease;
The Lord in my life provides me vision when I have no direction;
The Lord in my life extends his hand when I am lost;
The Lord in my life provides me relief when I thirst;
The Lord is always there for me. Without Him, I'm not me.
Thank you, Lord!

But they that wait upon the Lord shall renew their strength; they shall mount up with wings as eagles; they shall run, and not be weary; and they shall walk, and not faint. Isaiah 40:31

The Lord Knows the Difference

Church attendance
Once a month, every other week

Benevolent offering
Coins

Tithes and offering
Dollars

Evening Communion
Never

Evening services
Never

Special programs
Never

Play church, play church, play church
Play, play, play

Church attendance
Every week

Benevolent offering
Dollars

Tithes and Offering
Percentage of earnings

Evening Communion
Always

Evening services

Always

Special programs
Always

Pray church, pray church, pray church
Pray, pray, pray

The Lord knows the difference between play church and pray church.

The Lord is near to all who call upon Him, to all who call upon Him in truth. Psalm 145:18.

We Have Forgotten About God

Now that we have Lexus, Mercedes, and Cadillacs, we have
forgotten about God.
Now that we have elegant homes with well-kept lawns and decks,
we have forgotten about God.
Now that we have artifacts, paintings, and collectible dolls, we have
forgotten about God.
Now that we have steak and potatoes and chicken cordon bleu, we
have forgotten about God.
Now that we have wine, vodka, and black velvet, we have forgotten
about God.
Now that we have mink and leather coats and matching hats, we
have forgotten about God.
Now that we have diamonds, pearls, and birth stones, we have
forgotten about God.
Now that we have Nike, we have forgotten about God.
Now that we have maids, sitters, and beauticians, we have forgotten
about God.
Now that we have "The Young and the Restless," we have forgotten
about God.
Now that we have poodles, pek-a-poos and other toy dogs, we have
forgotten about God.

What if God had forgotten about us when we were in slavery?

Some trust in chariots, and some in horses; but we will remember
the name of the Lord our God. Psalm 20:7.

Who Am I?

I am my teddy bear's best friend.
I am my classmates' friend.
I am my mommy's baby.
I am my daddy's little boy.
I am my grandma's sunshine.
I am my grandpa's pride and joy.
I am my family's blessing.
I am God's child.

Written by Anthony Ephraim Patitu, II, at age five

Who Made God?

God made the flowers and trees.
God made the land and water.
God made the animals.
God made us.
Who made God?

Written by Anthony Ephraim Patitu, II, at age five

For by him were all things created, that are in heaven, and that
are in earth, visible and invisible, whether they be thrones, or
dominions, or principalities, or powers: all things were created by
him, and for him:
And he is before all things, and by him all things consist. Colossians
1: 16 – 17

But without faith it is impossible to please him; for he that cometh
to God must believe that he is, and that he is a rewarder of them
that diligently seek him. Hebrews 11: 6

RESPONSIBILITY

I Am Needed

I am needed by my mother;
I am needed by my father;
I am needed by my husband;
I am needed by my son;
I am needed by my pek-a-poo;
I am needed by my students;
I am needed by my friends;
I am needed by my community;
I am needed by my church;
I am needed by my siblings;
I am needed by my in-laws;
I am needed by little children; and
I am needed by people I don't know.
I am glad I am needed but to get me through it all, I need my God.

TIME

Changes

Nappy hair, curly hair
Permed hair, relaxed hair
Platts, braids, weave
Dark skin, bleached skin, natural skin
Hips, hips, and more hips
Nails with red polish, burgundy polish, brown polish
Lips painted red, burgundy, brown
Negro, Black, Afro-American, African American, Black
Then, Black and beautiful
Now, Black and beautiful
Changes

About The Author

Dr. Carol Logan Patitu is a Professor and Chairperson Pro-Tem in the Educational Foundations Department at Buffalo State (State University of New York). She works with the graduate program in Student Personnel Administration. All of 2000 she was a Fulbright Senior Scholar at the University of Durban-Westville in South Africa with the Faculty of Education. She earned her Ph.D. in Educational Administration and Supervision with an emphasis in higher education from Bowling Green State University. She holds both an Ed.S. and a M.Ed. in Student Personnel Services in Higher Education from the University of Florida and a B.A. in Secondary Education from Ohio Wesleyan University. She is a recipient of numerous awards. Dr. Patitu's research interests include student development, issues and concerns of minority students, and minority and women faculty in higher education, and she enjoys writing poetry. She has written articles and co-authored a book titled Faculty Job Satisfaction: Women and Minorities in Peril. She was a member of the Council for the International Exchange of Scholars U.S. Peer Review Committee for Southern Africa (South Africa, Zimbabwe, Botswana, Namibia, and Swaziland). She is an Associate Editor for Safundi: The Journal of South African & American Comparative Studies, and she has served as an associate editor and reviewer of other journals. She is President of the Western New York and Northwestern Pennsylvania Chapter of the Fulbright Association. She's also a member of the American College Personnel Association (ACPA) and the National Association for Student Personnel Administrators (NASPA), and she has been active in many other associations. She has conducted international and national presentations. She resides in Williamsville, New York with her husband Tony Ephraim Patitu and sons Anthony Ephraim Patitu, II, and Madiba Joseph Patitu.

ISBN 1412039797-7

9 781412 039796